Weather Watchers

STORMY

WRITTEN BY
Rebecca Phillips-Bartlett

KidHaven
PUBLISHING

Published in 2025 by
KidHaven Publishing, an Imprint of
Greenhaven Publishing, LLC
2544 Clinton St., Buffalo, NY 14224

Written by: Rebecca Phillips-Bartlett
Edited by: Elise Carraway
Designed by: Amelia Harris

Cataloging-in-Publication Data

Names: Phillips-Bartlett, Rebecca, 1999-.
Title: Stormy / Rebecca Phillips-Bartlett.
Description: Buffalo, New York : KidHaven Publishing, 2025. | Series: Weather watchers | Includes glossary and index.
Identifiers: ISBN 9781534547407 (pbk.) | ISBN 9781534547414 (library bound) | ISBN 9781534547421 (ebook)
Subjects: LCSH: Storms--Juvenile literature. | Climatic extremes--Juvenile literature. | Weather--Juvenile literature.
Classification: LCC QC941.3 P55 2025 | DDC 551.55--dc23

Manufactured in the United States of America

CPSIA compliance information: Batch #CSKH25
For further information contact Greenhaven Publishing LLC at 1-844-317-7404.

Please visit our website, www.greenhavenpublishing.com.
For a free color catalog of all our high-quality books, call toll free 1-844-317-7404 or fax 1-844-317-7405.

Find us on

IMAGE CREDITS

All images are courtesy of Shutterstock.com, unless otherwise specified. With thanks to Getty Images, Thinkstock Photo and iStockphoto.
Cover – behindlens, VikiVector, VectorDiploma, Oleh Svetiukha, Pogorelova Olga, fandijki, GoodStudio, Belozersky, FotoKina, a_v_d, 19 STUDIO, Heleno4ka. Character – Andrew Rybalko. 2–3 – GoodStudio, Kaspri, TORWAISTUDIO. 4–5 – John D Sirlin, Serg64, Tartila, Evgeny Atamanenko, Dmitry Demkin, DiKiYaqua, OoddySmile Studio, Ben Heys. 6–7 – Lester Balajadia, puifaiminiiz, Olga_Angelloz. 8–9 – Nikolay Zaborskikh, Eddy Savage, AlexanderTrou. 10–11 – Filippo Carlot, yevgeniy11, Oliver Hoffmann, DD2020. 12–13 – Triff, Bohdan Populov, OoddySmile Studio, Pau Buera. 14–15 – Huntstyle, dcwcreations, Aleutie, Iconic Bestiary. 16–17 – FotoKina, Mike Mareen, Ben Heys, behindlens. 18–19 – Sergey Nivens, Alan Budman, Kaspri. 20–21 – GoodStudio, TORWAISTUDIO, New Africa. 22–23 – Valentinka.ph, Roman Mikhailiuk.

CONTENTS

Words that look like **this** can be found in the glossary on page 24.

WHAT IS WEATHER?

My name is Mark. Thank you for tuning in to Weather Watchers TV. It is time to get you up to speed on what the weather is. Weather is what is happening in the air outside.

Look out of the window. What can you see?

I can see lots of dark, gray clouds outside. It looks like a storm is on the way...

STORMY WEATHER

A storm is a type of extreme weather. Storms often bring heavy rain and strong wind. Be careful your hat does not get blown away! Some storms even bring thunder and lightning.

There are many types of storms. Different parts of the world often have different storms. Most tornadoes happen in the middle of the U.S. Lots of thunderstorms happen in rainforests.

THUNDERSTORMS

It is very warm and humid here. That is the perfect weather for a thunderstorm to start. First, warm air rises up and causes clouds to form. In the clouds, a thunderstorm starts to grow.

Thunderclouds are full of tiny pieces of ice. These pieces of ice bump into each other. This creates lots of energy. That energy builds up until it makes a spark. That spark is called lightning.

LIGHTNING

Sometimes, lightning stays inside the cloud and lights up the sky. This is called sheet lightning. Sometimes, the lightning comes out of the cloud and reaches the ground. This is known as fork lightning.

Lightning makes the air very hot. It heats the air up to over 45,000 degrees Fahrenheit (25,000 degrees Celsius)! This heat causes a shock wave in the air. This wave makes the sound of thunder.

THUNDERSTORMS ARE ON THE WAY...

We normally see lightning before we hear thunder. This is because light moves faster than sound, so the light reaches us first. You can use this fact to figure out how far away a storm is.

The next time you see lightning, count how many seconds pass before you hear the thunder. The longer the gap, the farther away the storm is. The shorter the gap, the closer it is to you.

TORNADOES

Hold on tight! If the wind in a storm cloud is moving in certain directions, it can make a tornado. A tornado is a tube of air that goes from the cloud down to the ground.

The wind caused by a tornado can be very strong. It can move faster than a race car! Some tornadoes are so strong they destroy buildings and bridges. Others send leaves and branches flying.

HURRICANES

Hurricanes are another type of extreme storm. Hurricanes start over warm ocean waters. Most hurricanes happen out at sea where they do not cause much damage. However, when they reach land, they can cause big problems.

The wind in a hurricane moves around in a circle. The middle of a hurricane is called the eye. The eye is not windy. The eye wall is the windy and most dangerous part.

SAFE IN THE STORM

Storms can be scary! However, there are things you can do to stay safe. In a thunderstorm, it is safest to stay inside. If you are outside in a storm, avoid standing near trees.

If a hurricane or tornado is predicted, you will be told how to stay safe. If you are in an unexpected hurricane or tornado, find shelter. Stay as low as possible, such as in a basement.

SUPER STORMS

Sometimes, storms can be dangerous. However, a lot of the time, they play an important part in keeping the planet healthy. Thunderstorms often start after a period of dry, warm weather.

Thunderstorms help the planet cool down again. Thunderstorms also bring lots of rain. Plants need rain to grow. Without this rain, lots of plants and animals would not be able to live.

When the Storm Passes

Storms often do not last long. During a storm, make sure to follow the safety tips. After a storm, the air will be cooler, the plants will be watered, and you might see a rainbow!

Thank you for tuning in to Weather Watchers TV to learn all about what happens when the weather is stormy. Stay safe, and I will see you next time, once the storm has finally passed.

GLOSSARY

energy	a type of power, such as light or heat, that can be used to do something
extreme	much beyond what is normal or expected
Fahrenheit	a way of measuring temperature where water freezes at 32 degrees and boils at 212 degrees
flooding	when an area gets a lot more water than expected
humid	air containing a large amount of water
meteorologist	a scientist who studies the weather
predict	to make an educated guess about what will happen in the future
shelter	a place to stay safe from bad weather or danger
tornado	a strong storm that creates a funnel of strong wind

INDEX